Follett Coping Skills Series
Job Interviews

Developed by
McVey & Associates, Inc.

Reading Consultant
Daniel T. Fishco, Ed.D.
Director, Institutional Development Programs
Yavapai College
Prescott, Arizona

Educational Consultant
Joanne Dembinski
Supervisor, Michigan Life Role Competencies Project
Pontiac Public Schools
Pontiac, Michigan

CAMBRIDGE Adult Education
Prentice Hall Regents, Englewood Cliffs, NJ 07632

Published and distributed by:

Cambridge, The Adult Education Company
888 Seventh Avenue
New York, NY 10106

ISBN: 0-8428-2329-8
(Originally published by Follett Publishing Company as ISBN: 0-695-22180-9)

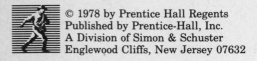
© 1978 by Prentice Hall Regents
Published by Prentice-Hall, Inc.
A Division of Simon & Schuster
Englewood Cliffs, New Jersey 07632

Printed in the United States of America

10 9 8 7 6 5 4 3 2 1

ISBN 0-8428-2329-8 01

Prentice-Hall International (UK) Limited, *London*
Prentice-Hall of Australia Pty. Limited, *Sydney*
Prentice-Hall Canada Inc., *Toronto*
Prentice-Hall Hispanoamericana, S.A., *Mexico*
Prentice-Hall of India Private Limited, *New Delhi*
Prentice-Hall of Japan, Inc., *Tokyo*
Simon & Schuster Asia Pte. Ltd., *Singapore*
Editora Prentice-Hall do Brasil, Ltda., *Rio de Janeiro*

CONTENTS

Setting Up a Job Interview

Let's say you want a job. You know what kind of job you want. You can do that kind of job. And you know about places with open jobs. What should you do next?

You should set up a job interview at each place. A job interview is a meeting about getting a job. Three important things happen at a job interview.

1. You learn about the job.
2. You learn about the employer. An employer is a person or business that hires people for jobs. Governments are employers, too.
3. The interviewer learns about you. An interviewer is a person you talk to about a job.

A job interview helps you decide if you want the job. It helps you decide if you can do the job. A job interview is important to the interviewer, too. It helps the interviewer decide if you should be hired. A good interview can help you get a job.

This lesson is about setting up a job interview. Other lessons are about things you can do to have good interviews.

Lisa Cole works in a factory. She works from four o'clock in the afternoon to midnight. Lisa goes to school in the morning. She takes typing. She wants a job in an office. Lisa knows about places that have open jobs. She wants to set up job interviews at these places.

Lisa decides to phone one company. She knows about an open job at the company. She phones the personnel office of the company. The people who work for an employer are personnel. A personnel office is often in charge of hiring people. On page 6 you can read about Lisa's phone call. Lisa spoke to Mr. Edwards in the personnel office.

Mr. Edwards. Hello. This is the personnel office. May I help you?

Lisa. Hello. I would like to talk to someone about the typing job that is open.

Mr. Edwards. I can set up an interview for you. May I have your name?

Lisa. Yes. My name is Lisa Cole.

Mr. Edwards. May I have your phone number, too?

Lisa. My phone number is 555-1645.

Mr. Edwards. Can you come for an interview tomorrow morning at nine o'clock?

Lisa. Yes. That time is fine.

Mr. Edwards. Come to the Clark Coat Company. The personnel office is at 419 West May Street. The office is in room 125. You will talk to Mrs. Herrod.

Lisa. Thank you. I will be there at nine.

Mr. Edwards was very helpful. He gave Lisa information about the interview. Lisa had paper and a pen so she could write down the information.

What information did Lisa get about the interview? Answer these questions about Lisa's telephone call. Write your answers in the blanks.

1. What day is Lisa's interview? _____*tomorrow morning*_____

2. What time is Lisa's interview? _____*nine o'clock*_____

3. What is the name of the company? _*Clark coat campany*_

4. What is the address of the personnel office? _*419 west May street.*_

_____

5. In what room is the personnel office? _*The office is in room 125*_

6. What is the name of the interviewer? _*The name is Mrs. Herrod.*_

Turn to page 60 and check your answers.

Lisa set up her interview over the phone. A telephone call is one way to set up an interview. You might set up an interview over the phone for these reasons.

- You hear about an open job from a friend. You want to check with the company. You want to make sure the job is still open.

- You live far away from the company. It is easier to call than to go to the company.

- You read about the job in a help wanted ad. A help wanted ad is a job listed in a newspaper or magazine. The ad tells you to call for an interview.

Lisa's friend George Davis also set up an interview over the phone. A friend told George about an open job. George phoned the company. He asked a man in the personnel office about the job. The man told George to come for an interview in two hours. Then the man hung up the phone.

George did not get all the information he needed. He found out only the time of the interview. George should have asked more questions about the interview.

Read the questions below. Put an X in front of each question George should have asked.

___X__1. What is the address of the company?

_____2. Will the interview be held at this address?

___X__3. In what room will the interview be held?

___X__4. Who will I speak to about the job?

You should have put an X in front of all the questions. George needed all of this information. You should have this information about each interview you set up.

Look at Form 1 below. It has a list of things you need to know about a job interview. Make copies of Form 1. Use one copy for each job interview. Get the information from the person you talk to when you set up an interview. Write the information in the blanks. Then you won't forget the information.

Interview Information—Form 1

NAME OF EMPLOYER _____

ADDRESS OF EMPLOYER _____

ADDRESS WHERE INTERVIEW WILL BE HELD (IF DIFFERENT) _____

_____

PHONE NUMBER OF EMPLOYER _____

DATE OF INTERVIEW _____

TIME OF INTERVIEW _____

NAME OF INTERVIEWER _____

OFFICE OR ROOM WHERE INTERVIEW WILL BE HELD _____

Lisa and George used the telephone to set up interviews. But you might set up an interview in person. You might set up an interview in person for these reasons.

- You see a sign. It is in front of a company's office. The sign lists an open job. You go into the office. You ask about the job.
- You read about a job in a help wanted ad. The ad says that people should go to the company. The ad says to come in person for an interview.

Keep a copy of Form 1 with you. You can use it if you set up an interview in person. You can write down the information about the interview.

Checking Facts from the Lesson

Put an X in front of each correct statement.

_____1. You can set up some job interviews over the phone.

_____2. You call to set up interviews. The people you talk to will give you information. You do not have to ask questions.

_____3. A job interview helps the interviewer. But the interview does not help you.

_____4. A help wanted ad may tell you to phone for an interview.

Using Words from the Lesson

Write the correct words in the blanks below. Use these words.

job interview   employer
personnel office   interviewer

1. You work for the Jacobs Company. The company is your
_____*employer*_____.

2. A person talks to you and asks you questions at an interview. This person is an _____*interviewer*_____.

3. A _____*personnel office*_____ is often in charge of hiring people.

4. A meeting about getting a job is a _____*job interview*_____.

Drawing Conclusions

Write Yes or No in front of each question.

___*No*___1. You set up an interview over the phone. The person does not tell you the time of the interview. Does this mean that the time is not important?

___*Yes*___2. You go to work for your uncle. He owns a restaurant. Is your uncle your employer?

___*Yes*___3. You read a help wanted ad. It says to go to the company for an interview. The ad gives a phone number. But it does not give an address. Should you call to get the address?

___*Yes*___4. You go to a company to set up an interview. The person you talk to gives you most of the information you need. But the person does not tell you the name of the interviewer. Should you ask for the information?

Turn to page 61 and check your answers.

Information You Need for an Interview

You have set up a job interview. Your next step is to get ready for the interview. You must plan to get to the place. And you should learn about the employer.

You also need to put together information about yourself. Information about yourself is personal information. The information will help you answer questions about yourself.

This lesson will help you get ready for an interview. It will help you put together some information you will need.

Important Words Used in This Lesson

application An application is a spoken or written request for a job.

services Services are work done for people. A doctor gives medical services. A house painter gives painting services.

Social Security Social Security is a United States government program. It pays money because of retirement, disability, or death. It pays money when income is reduced. You must have a Social Security number to get a job.

Getting to the Interview

You know where you will have the interview. You should find out how to get to the place. And you need to know how long it takes to get there. The employer may be far from your home. You should be sure you could get to the job each day. If you are not sure, you should not go for an interview. You should not take the job.

You should plan how you will get to each interview. It is good to leave early for an interview. Then you will arrive on time. This shows the interviewer that you are reliable. Reliable means you can be depended on. Interviewers like reliable people.

It is good to show an interviewer that you know something about the company. Your interest shows that you care about the company and the job. Your interest can help you get the job.

Find out some things about an employer before you go to an interview. Then you can talk to the interviewer about those things. Form 2 below lists some important information you might get. Make a few copies of the form. Fill out a form before each job interview you have.

You may not find all the information for the form. Find as much as you can. You may phone for an interview. Then you can ask some questions when you set up the interview. Or you may have a friend who works for the employer. You can ask the friend about the employer.

Employer Information—Form 2

Name of employer _____

Address of employer _____

Does the employer manufacture things? Manufacture means make. _____

What does the employer manufacture? _____

_____

Does the employer give services? _____

What are the services? _____

_____

How many people work for the employer? _____

What are the working hours? _____

How many plants, offices, or stores does the employer have? _____

What else do you know about the employer? _____

_____

_____

_____

Personal Information

Interviewers want to know certain things about you. An interviewer will probably ask you questions about yourself. Questions about yourself are personal questions.

Interviewers also get information about you from a job application form. You fill out a job application form when you apply for a job. Apply means ask for or try out for something, like a job. A job application form usually has questions about these things.

- Personal information. Personal information is information about yourself. Your name, telephone number, address, and Social Security number are personal information.

- Education. Education means where and when you went to school. It also means how many years of school you have had.

- Job experience. Job experience means a list of the places where you have worked. It also means the kinds of work you have done.

- References. References are people who know you well. They can give information about you. But they should not be members of your family or your friends. Your teacher or doctor can be a reference. An employer can be a reference. Other people can be references, too. You will need the names, addresses, and phone numbers of your references.

- Hobbies. Hobbies are things you like to do on your own. Some hobbies might help you do a job.

Have your personal information ready before the interview. Form 3 on page 13 is a personal information form. You can make a copy of it. Fill in as much information as you can. You can take the form to the job interview. Then you will be able to answer many of the questions you may be asked.

Personal Information—Form 3

PERSONAL INFORMATION

NAME _____ TELEPHONE _____

ADDRESS _____ CITY _____

STATE _____ ZIP _____ SOCIAL SECURITY NUMBER _____

EDUCATION

	NAME OF SCHOOL	ADDRESS	DATES FROM	TO	DID YOU GRADUATE? (FINISH)
ELEMENTARY	_____	_____	____	____	_____
JR. HIGH	_____	_____	____	____	_____
HIGH SCHOOL	_____	_____	____	____	_____
VOCATIONAL (JOB TRAINING)	_____	_____	____	____	_____
BUSINESS OR TRADE SCHOOL	_____	_____	____	____	_____
COLLEGE	_____	_____	____	____	_____
OTHER	_____	_____	____	____	_____

JOB EXPERIENCE

NAME OF COMPANY	ADDRESS	WORK YOU DID	DATES FROM	TO	SALARY
_____	_____	_____	____	____	____
_____	_____	_____	____	____	____
_____	_____	_____	____	____	____
_____	_____	_____	____	____	____

REFERENCES

NAME	ADDRESS	PHONE	OCCUPATION
_____	_____	_____	_____
_____	_____	_____	_____
_____	_____	_____	_____

HOBBIES

_____

_____

Checking Facts from the Lesson

Put an X in front of each correct statement.

_____1. You should get some information about an employer before a job interview.

_____2. It is helpful to write down personal information at home before an interview.

_____3. You should be sure you could get to a place every day. You should be sure before you go to the interview.

_____4. It doesn't help to know ahead of time how to get to an interview.

Using Words from the Lesson

Write the correct words in the blanks below. Use these words.

references   job application
services   manufacture

1. You usually fill out a _____ form when you apply for a job.

2. _____ are people who can give information about you to employers.

3. _____ are work done for people.

4. _____ means to make something.

Drawing Conclusions

Write Yes or No in front of each question.

_____1. One of your high school teachers knows you well. Your last employer liked your work. Might these people be good references?

_____2. You have an interview at a food plant. The company makes more than fifty kinds of foods. Would it be good for you to know what some of the foods are?

_____3. You don't remember the dates when you worked at your old jobs. You do not want to call the places to get the dates. You go to the interview without the information. Is this a good thing to do?

_____4. A friend tells you about an open job where she works. You set up an interview for the job. Is it a good idea to ask her for some information about the company before you have the interview?

Turn to page 61 and check your answers.

Lesson 3

Dressing to Get a Job

Sandra Johnson wants to work for a laundry. She wants to be a driver. She would pick up and deliver clothes. Sandra has the qualifications for the job. A qualification is anything that makes you able to do a job. Being able to drive is one qualification for the delivery job Sandra wants.

Sandra talks to a friend who is a driver for another laundry. She asks her friend what the drivers wear. The friend tells her. Women wear pants and blouses. Sometimes they wear jackets. They wear low-heeled shoes. The women do not wear a lot of jewelry. Men wear shirts, pants, and plain shoes. Sometimes the men wear jackets, too.

Sandra goes to her interview. She wears dark blue pants, a white blouse, and low-heeled shoes. She wears a silver necklace and a watch. Sandra Johnson gets the job. Why? One reason is that she has the qualifications for the job. Another reason is the way she looks. The interviewer can see that Sandra cares. She cares about how she looks. She cares about getting the job. Sandra knows what kind of clothes are good for the job.

This lesson is about how to dress for a job interview. It shows you that how you dress can help you get the job.

Important Words Used in This Lesson

appearance Appearance is how someone or something looks. Your appearance is made up of many things. Your hair and your clothes are part of your appearance. How you sit and walk are part of your appearance.

Interviewers do not have much time to get to know you. Your appearance helps them decide if you should get the job. Think about the job you want. Try to dress right for that job. For example, a secretary wears different clothes than a shipping clerk. You may want to find out how people dress for the job you want. This is what Sandra Johnson did.

People may wear uniforms for the job you want. Uniforms are special clothes some people must wear when they work. Nurses wear uniforms. Police officers wear uniforms. But you should not wear a uniform to a job interview.

You can dress up a little for an interview. Let's say a job for an auto mechanic is open. Men and women could wear neat work clothes to an interview for this job. But a woman could wear a skirt and blouse. A man could wear a sports jacket and tie. You should not get too dressed up. The interviewer may think you are not thinking about the job.

Always look neat and clean when you go to an interview. Maybe you will get dirty when you work. You should still look neat and clean at an interview. A neat, clean appearance says that you care. You care about yourself. You care about getting the job. These are important things to show an interviewer.

Below is a list of some things that make up your appearance. You may want to check these things before an interview.

Clothes	Should be clean, neat, and simple. No missing buttons or untidy hems. Iron your clothes if necessary. Shoes should be clean and shiny. The heels should not be run down.
Hair	Should be clean and combed. Fancy hairstyles are not necessary.
Beard or mustache	Should be clean and short.
Fingernails	Should be clean and short. Nail polish is OK if it is neat and a light color.
Makeup	Should be simple and light.
Jewelry	Should be simple. It is better to wear very little jewelry.
Perfume	Should not be strong.
Coat	Take off your outdoor coat at an interview. Hang it up or put it over the back of your chair. Or hold it on your lap.
Hat	Take off your hat at an interview.
Sunglasses	Take off your sunglasses at an interview.

You will read about two people who have job interviews. They are Cynthia Ayala and Allan Partee. Cynthia and Allan want different kinds of jobs. Each of them has the qualifications for the job. Their appearance can help them. Or their appearance can hurt their chances of getting the job. Read the information about each person. Put an X in front of the correct answer to each question. Then turn to page 60 and check your answers.

Cynthia Ayala

Cynthia Ayala applies for a job as a nurse's aide in a hospital. She goes to the interview. Cynthia's skirt is very short. She wears shoes with very high heels. Her shoes make a lot of noise when she walks. She has long fingernails.

Does Cynthia look like a nurse's aide?   ____Yes   _X_No

Will her appearance help her get the job?   ____Yes   _✓_No

Allan Partee

Allan Partee applies for a job as a salesclerk in a camera store. He goes to the store for an interview. Allan wears a suit. He wears brown shoes with low heels. A watch and one ring are the only jewelry he wears. His hair is neat. His hands are clean.

Does Allan look like a salesclerk?   ____Yes   ____No

Will his appearance help him get the job?   ____Yes   ____No

Turn to page 60 and check your answers.

Checking Facts from the Lesson

Put an X in front of each correct statement.

X 1. A neat appearance may help you get a job.

___2. You should keep your outdoor coat on during an interview.

X 3. It is better for people to wear very little jewelry to interviews.

___4. The clothing you wear to a job interview is not important.

Using Words from the Lesson

Write the correct words in the blanks below. Use these words.

appearance   qualifications
applies   uniforms

1. Your _____appearance_____ is the way you look.

2. People wear _____uniforms_____ for some kinds of jobs.

3. A person who _____applies_____ for a job should think about how to dress for the interview.

4. A neat appearance may help you get a job. You also need to have the _____qualification_____ for the job.

Drawing Conclusions

Write Yes or No in front of each question.

No 1. Tony has an interview. He wants to be a janitor in a factory. Is a suit the only kind of clothing he could wear to the interview?

No 2. You apply for a job as an auto mechanic. Auto mechanics often have car oil on their hands. Their clothes get dirty at work. Does this mean that you do not have to try to be neat and clean at the interview?

Yes 3. You started to grow a beard two days ago. It does not look very neat. You have a job interview today. Should you shave your beard before the interview?

Yes 4. Nancy likes to wear skirts more than she likes to wear pants. She applies for a factory job. Is it all right for Nancy to wear a plain skirt to the interview?

Turn to page 61 and check your answers.

What to Expect from an Interviewer

Juan Galvez went to two job interviews last week. One interviewer was very friendly. He asked Juan many questions about himself. Juan and the interviewer talked for a long time. The other interviewer was not very friendly. She asked Juan about his job experience. Then she ended the interview.

Interviewers are different. Some will be friendly. Others will not be so friendly. Some interviewers will ask many questions. Others will ask only a few.

But all interviewers need information about you. This lesson is about some things interviewers want to know.

Important Words Used in This Lesson

benefit A benefit is an extra thing you get besides your pay. You may get benefits from a company you work for. Paid insurance is a benefit. Vacation pay is a benefit.

skill A skill is something you know how to do because you have training or experience. Typing is a skill. Running a drill press is a skill. Driving a truck is a skill.

All interviewers do not act the same. Juan's interviewers were very different. But Juan didn't care. He knew that all interviewers are looking for good people to fill jobs. How an interviewer acts is not important. How Juan acts is important. Juan must show the interviewer that he could do the job well.

An interviewer needs to know why you should be hired instead of someone else. An interviewer may also want to know why you want to work for the employer.

The interviewer may ask you for this information. Or the interviewer may want you to talk about these things on your own. You must show the interviewer that the employer should hire you. You must show the interviewer that you want to work for the employer.

Now you will read some questions an interviewer may ask. Two answers are given for each question. Choose the better answer. The better answer is the one that shows that you are a good person to hire.

Interview for a Job in a Shipping Department

Interviewer. Good morning. Nice day, isn't it? Great day to be fishing. Now, let's see. I read about your last job on your application. What work did you do?

Read the two answers below. Put an X in front of the better answer.

_____1. I worked with five other people on my last job. We wrapped pictures for shipping. We had to find the best way to wrap each picture. Sometimes we chose the best way to ship each picture, too.

_____2. I didn't do much on my last job. I just wrapped things. There was not much to the job.

The first answer is the better one. It tells the interviewer about your work. It shows that the job was important to you. Interviewers like to hear these things. They show that you are a good worker.

Interview for a Job with an Air-conditioning Service

Interviewer. I've read your application. I don't think that you have done this kind of work before. What makes you think you can fix air conditioners?

Read the two answers below. Put an X in front of the better answer.

_____1. I've had lots of jobs before. I never had any problem doing a job. I even took a class. I learned a little about air conditioners.

_____2. I know how to fix many machines. Last summer I went to a special school. I learned how to fix air conditioners. I did well in my class. You can talk to the teacher, Mr. Sams. He will tell you about my work.

The second answer is the better one. It tells the interviewer what skills you have. You give the interviewer a reference, too. The interviewer can ask the teacher about you. Your answer helps the interviewer know that you could do a good job.

Reasons to Work for a Certain Employer

The interviewer may ask you why you want to work for <u>this</u> employer. Do you have good reasons? Tell the interviewer your reasons. This information may help you get the job. But give only the reasons that are true.

You might want to work for a certain employer for these reasons.

- You like the employer's products or services. Products are things a company makes or grows. Cars are a product. Canned peas are a product. Services are work done for people. A plumber gives services. An auto mechanic gives services.
- You have heard that the employer treats employees well. Employees are people who work for a person or company.
- You know the employer pays well.
- You know the employer gives good benefits.
- You could get to work easily. The employer is close to your home.

Reasons for an Employer to Hire You

Sometimes an interviewer will ask you why you should be hired. You should be ready to give an answer.

Here are some reasons an employer might hire you. You should tell these reasons to the interviewer. But tell them only if the reasons are true.

- You have the skills to do the job.
- You are a hard worker.
- You are a fast learner.
- You are reliable.
- You are willing to learn how to do new things.
- You get along well with people.

Checking Facts from the Lesson

Put an <u>X</u> in front of each correct statement.

_____1. All interviewers act the same way at job interviews.

_____2. Interviewers may ask you why you should be hired.

_____3. Interviewers may not ask a lot of questions.

_____4. It is good to tell an interviewer that you are reliable.

_____5. Interviewers are always friendly.

Using Words from the Lesson

Write the correct words in the blanks below. Use these words.

products   employees
benefit   skill

1. Vacation pay is a job ___benifit___.

2. Things that a company makes or grows to sell are ___products___.

3. Something you can do because you have training or experience is a ___skill___.

4. ___employees___ are people who work for an employer.

Drawing Conclusions

Write <u>Yes</u> or <u>No</u> in front of each question.

___Yes___1. You have an interview at the Pearl Furniture Company. The company is only six blocks from your home. You could walk to work easily. Is this a good thing to tell the interviewer?

_____2. The interviewer does not seem sure that you have the skills for the job. Your last employer can be a good reference. The employer can tell the interviewer about your skills. Should you tell the interviewer about the employer?

___Yes___3. The interviewer does not ask about special skills you have. But your skills will help you do the job. Is it a good idea to tell the interviewer about them?

_____4. You go to a job interview. The interviewer says she is very busy that morning. She only talks to you for five minutes. Does this mean you will not get the job?

Turn to page 62 and check your answers.

What to Do at a Job Interview

Harry Adams has a job interview at 9:30 A.M. Harry's brother drives him to the company. He goes into the building with Harry.

The two men walk into the personnel office. They talk loud and tell jokes. Then the interviewer calls Harry into her office. Harry's brother tells him not to worry. He waves his hand and smiles at the interviewer.

Harry and the interviewer sit down in her office. Harry has his interview. Then Harry comes out of the office. Harry and his brother talk about the interview as they leave the office.

Harry thinks the interview went well. He may be right. But he may <u>not</u> get the job.

This lesson will tell you why Harry may not get the job. The lesson tells about some things you <u>should</u> do at an interview. And it tells about some things you <u>should not</u> do at an interview.

Important Words Used in This Lesson

impression An impression is the feeling you give people about yourself. Many things make an impression. Your appearance makes an impression. How you act makes an impression. You want to make a good impression on the interviewer.

Harry may not get the job. He brought someone with him to the interview. This is not a good thing to do. The interviewer may think you cannot do anything by yourself. Harry and his brother were talking loud. You should be quiet in the personnel office. You should not laugh and talk too much. Being loud does not make a good impression.

There are other things that don't make a good impression at an interview. And there are things that do make a good impression. Making a good impression can help you get the job.

You will read about two people who have job interviews. Read the information about each person. Answer the questions that follow the information. Write your answers in the blanks.

Ana Cantu

Ana Cantu wants a job as a bookkeeper. She has worked as a bookkeeper before. Ana has written down the personal information she needs. She brings this to the interview. She also brings her Social Security card. Ana also has her driver's license. If she gets the job, she may have to prove her age. The driver's license shows her age. Ana is prepared for her interview.

What three important things does Ana bring to the interview?

1. _____

2. _____

3. _____

Will Ana probably make a good impression? _____

Why? _____

Ana brings her personal information, her Social Security card, and her driver's license. Ana will probably make a good impression. Why? Because she is prepared for the interview.

Paul Kim

Paul Kim likes to read. He applies for a job in the library. The job is to put books in the right place. Paul gets to the interview fifteen minutes early. He throws away his chewing gum. He sits down and waits for his interview.

Paul does two good things. They will help his chances for getting the job. What are they?

1. _____

2. _____

Paul gets to the interview early. This shows the interviewer that he is reliable. Paul throws away his chewing gum. He can talk more clearly without gum in his mouth.

There are things you should do if you have a job interview. And there are things you should not do if you have a job interview. On page 27 are two short lists. The information in the lists will help you have better interviews.

Things You Should Do If You Have a Job Interview

1. Do phone the interviewer if you cannot go to the interview. Ask if you can change the interview to a different time. Do this only if you have a real problem, like being sick.

2. Do get a good night's sleep before the interview. You will feel more awake. You will be able to make a better impression.

3. Do get to the interview early. This shows that you are reliable. It shows that you will probably be a reliable employee. And you may worry less about the interview if you arrive early.

4. Do take off your hat and outdoor coat.

5. Do know how to say the interviewer's name. This makes the interviewer feel good. Maybe the name is hard to say. Ask the interviewer how to say it.

6. Do shake hands with the interviewer. People often shake hands at an interview. You shake hands when the interview starts. You also shake hands when the interview ends.

7. Do sit up straight. You will probably look more interested in the interview and the job.

8. Do look at the interviewer when you talk. This shows that you are sure of yourself.

Things You Should Not Do If You Have a Job Interview

1. Don't sit down in the interviewer's office until the interviewer asks you to.

2. Don't call the interviewer by his or her first name. Use the person's last name. Say Mrs. Levy or Mr. Stevenson, for example.

3. Don't look at your watch during the interview. The interviewer will think you do not want to spend much time at the interview.

4. Don't smoke at the interview. The interviewer might not like smoking. Maybe the company does not allow smoking at work. But what if the interviewer says that you may smoke? You still should not smoke.

5. Don't wear sunglasses. The interviewer wants to look at your whole face. The interviewer cannot see your whole face when you wear sunglasses.

6. Don't talk while the interviewer is reading your application. The interviewer may have trouble reading if you talk.

7. Don't ask right away about pay, working hours, or benefits. Wait until the interviewer brings up these things. Then you can ask questions. It is better to discuss your qualifications and experience first.

Checking Facts from the Lesson

Put an X in front of each correct statement.

_____1. You can call the interviewer by his or her first name. You can do this as soon as you meet the interviewer.

_____2. You should phone the interviewer if you cannot come to the interview.

_____3. You usually shake hands with the interviewer.

_____4. You should begin a job interview by asking about the pay.

Using Words from the Lesson

Write the correct words in the blanks below. Use these words.

impression   interviewer
prepared   Social Security

1. You bring your personal information to the interview. This will help you

   be _____.

2. It is easier to make a good _____ when you are prepared for an interview.

3. An _____ talks to you about a job.

4. _____ is a United States government program.

Drawing Conclusions

Write Yes or No in front of each question.

_____1. You have a problem with your eyes. The doctor told you to wear sunglasses for two weeks. You go to a job interview. You have to wear your sunglasses. Should you tell the interviewer what your doctor said?

_____2. Your son is sick. You cannot get to a job interview on time. You go to the interview two hours late. Is this a good thing to do?

_____3. A friend gives you a ride to your job interview. She is going to wait for you. She will be angry if you stay too long. Should you tell the interviewer that you cannot spend a lot of time at the interview?

Turn to page 62 and check your answers.

Lesson 6

Questions You May Be Asked

Interviewers will ask you questions. They usually want certain kinds of information from you. For example, most interviewers will ask about your qualifications for a job.

Your answers are important. Some answers are better than others. Better answers may help <u>you</u> get the job instead of someone else.

This lesson tells about some questions you may be asked. It will help you answer the questions better.

Important Words Used in This Lesson

---

goal A goal is something you try to get. Or it is something you try to do. Your goal may be to get a new coat. Your goal may be to finish school.

promotion A promotion is a better job in the same company. What happens if you get a promotion? You may earn more money. You may do more important work. Or you may direct other people's work. Someone who directs other people's work is a supervisor.

Questions About Your Job Qualifications

The interviewer will probably ask about your job qualifications. You may be asked these questions.

- What kinds of work do you like to do?
- What kinds of work do you do well?
- What are your qualifications for this job?

Some of these questions may be on the job application. But the interviewer wants to hear you talk about your skills and experience.

You should think about your qualifications and skills <u>before</u> you have an interview. Let's say you apply for a job in the order department of a company. You worked as a supply clerk in the army. You could use your skills to do the job. Be ready to tell about your work.

You may apply for a job that has been filled. But the company may have other open jobs. Maybe you have the skills for one of the open jobs. Be ready to tell an interviewer about all your skills and qualifications.

Here is another question the interviewer may ask. Two answers are given for the question. Put an <u>X</u> in front of the better answer.

Interviewer. What skills did you learn from your last job?

_____ 1. I learned to do a lot of things.

_____ 2. I learned to run a copy machine. I learned how to take orders over the phone. I also learned how to fill orders.

Turn to page 60 and check your answer.

Questions About Your Work Record

The interviewer may ask questions about your work record. Your work record is information about the jobs you have had. The information is about the kind of work you did. How long you stayed at other jobs is part of your work record. How well you did your work is also part of your work record. Some of this information will be asked for on the job application. But the interviewer may also ask you these questions.

- What was your last job like?
- Were you treated well at your last job?
- May we call your old employer? May we ask about you?

The interviewer wants to find out several things. Are you a hard worker? Did you get along well with people at work? Tell the truth. Maybe you had a problem. Let's say you were fired. You did not get along with your supervisor. But you have learned from your mistake. You can tell the interviewer this. Maybe you quit a job or were laid off. A job might have been too hard or too easy.

You should tell the interviewer the truth. The interviewer can check your record. But tell the interviewer why you want the job. Tell the interviewer what you can do <u>now</u>.

Here is another question the interviewer may ask. Put an X in front of the best answer.

Interviewer. Why did you leave your last job?

_____1. I didn't like the people there.

_____2. The job was boring.

_____3. I want to work where I can get a promotion. My old company did not give many promotions.

Turn to page 60 and check your answer.

Questions About Your Future Plans

The interviewer may ask questions about your plans for the future. Here are some questions you may be asked.

- What are your vocational plans? Vocational plans are work plans.
- Are there other jobs you would like to learn to do?
- What are your goals for the next few years?

The interviewer wants to find out if you are interested in doing this kind of work. Maybe you will be interested in doing other jobs at the place. The interviewer wants to find out if you will be a good employee. Be ready to answer questions about your future plans.

Let's say you are having an interview for a job in a factory. The factory is in a city. The interviewer asks you the question below. Put an X in front of the better answer.

Interviewer. What are your goals for the next few years?

_____ 1. I don't like this city. I want to move to another state as soon as I can.

_____ 2. I would like to get into your training program. Then I could learn more skills.

Turn to page 60 and check your answer.

Other Questions You May Be Asked

Here are some other questions you may be asked. Some of the questions may be asked on the job application. Or the interviewer may ask you the questions.

- What education do you have? Do you have any special job training?
- What are your hobbies?
- Can you work overtime? Overtime means extra hours.
- How much money did you make on your last job?
- What salary do you want? A salary is money you get for doing a regular job.

Try to think of other questions you may be asked. Think about your answers. Then you can have a better job interview.

Checking Facts from the Lesson

Put an X in front of each correct statement.

_____1. Most interviewers want to know about your job qualifications.

_____2. Your work record is not important to interviewers.

_____3. A job interviewer may ask about your hobbies.

_____4. You were fired from a job. You should not tell this to an interviewer.

_____5. An interviewer wants to know what work you like to do.

Using Words from the Lesson

Write the correct words in the blanks below. Use these words.

promotion   supervisor
goal   salary

1. Your _____ may be to buy a car.

2. You get a better job in the same company. This is a

_____.

3. A _____ directs other people's work.

4. A _____ is money you get for doing a job.

Drawing Conclusions

Write Yes or No in front of each question.

_____1. At your last job, you found a way to do the work faster. The company used your idea. Should you tell this to an interviewer?

_____2. The interviewer asks you about your work plans. You are interested in the work and would like more training. But you tell the interviewer that you have no plans. Is this a good answer?

_____3. You want a job working with older people. Your grandmother lived with you for fifteen years. You helped take care of her. Should you tell this to an interviewer?

_____4. The interviewer asks you what salary you think you should get. You say that you did not think about the salary. Is this a good answer?

Turn to page 62 and check your answers.

Lesson 7

Answering the Hard Questions

It may not be easy to answer all the questions an interviewer asks. You may have to think about <u>how</u> you will answer some questions. You may have a problem that will hurt your chances of getting a job. For example, maybe you do not have many job skills. Or maybe you dropped out of school.

This lesson tells about some people who have problems. These people must find good ways to answer some questions. They must tell the truth. But they must also show why they should be hired for the job.

Sarah Jenkins

Sarah Jenkins was arrested when she was nineteen. She was arrested for stealing clothes from a store. Sarah was convicted by a court. Convicted means found guilty. So Sarah has a conviction on her record.

Sarah has a job interview at a grocery store. She wants to be a checker. A checker takes care of money. People pay the checker for groceries.

The interviewer asks Sarah this question.

Interviewer. Have you ever been convicted of a crime?

Choose the answer you think Sarah should give. Put an <u>X</u> in front of the answer you choose.

_____1. Yes. I was convicted of stealing clothes.

_____2. No. I was never convicted of a crime.

_____3. Yes. I was convicted of stealing clothes when I was nineteen. But I learned my lesson. Nothing like that has happened again. And it won't happen in the future.

The third answer is the one Sarah should give. Sarah tells the truth about her conviction. But she tells the interviewer other things. She says that she learned from her mistake. Sarah tells the interviewer that it won't happen again. She shows that she will be a good employee.

The second answer is a bad answer. Sarah might be hired for the job. But the interviewer can check Sarah's record. Sarah could be fired later because she lied.

David Lowe

David Lowe has not had a full-time job for five years. He has had some part-time jobs. David does not have any special job skills.

David has a job interview. He wants to load trucks for a moving company.

The interviewer asks David some questions.

Interviewer. I've read your application. You haven't had a full-time job for five years. Why not? Why should I hire you for <u>this</u> job?

Choose the answer you think David should give. Put an <u>X</u> in front of the answer you choose.

_____1. Nobody wants to hire me for a full-time job. I don't have any skills.

_____2. I don't have the special skills that are needed for most jobs. So some companies don't want to hire me. But I work hard. And I am reliable. You can check the places I worked part-time. I can do the job you have. And I want a full-time job. I just need the chance to show you what I can do.

_____3. I don't really want a full-time job. I just want some money. I want enough money to keep going.

The second answer is the one David should give. He tells the truth about his skills. But he tells the interviewer other things. He says he works hard. David says he wants a full-time job. And he says that the interviewer can check with his old employers. David gives the interviewer some good reasons to hire him.

The other answers are not good. They do not tell the interviewer why David should be hired. The other answers do not show that David would be a good worker.

Natalie Daniels

Natalie Daniels is twenty-four. She did not finish high school. She dropped out when she was a junior. Natalie has worked since she dropped out of high school. She has eight years of work experience.

Natalie has a job interview at a factory. She wants to put together parts of television sets. Natalie has not done this work before. But she has had other jobs. She has done work that is almost the same as this.

The interviewer asks Natalie this question.

Interviewer. Did you finish high school?

Choose the answer you think Natalie should give. Put an X in front of the answer you choose.

_____1. No. I dropped out when I was a junior.

_____2. No. I dropped out when I was a junior. But I have been working for eight years. My other employers will give me good references. And I have experience from other jobs. I think I could do this job very well.

_____3. Yes. I finished high school.

The second answer is the one Natalie should give. Natalie tells the truth about her education. She also tells the interviewer about her good work record. She says that she has good references. Natalie tells about her experience, too. She gives some good reasons that she should be hired.

The third answer is a bad one. Natalie should not lie about her education. The interviewer can check her record.

Pete Andrews

Pete Andrews used some drugs when he was in high school. He and some friends took pills at parties. They thought it would be fun to take the pills. But Pete didn't like the way the drugs made him feel. He stopped taking the pills. Pete has not used any drugs in five years.

Pete has a job interview at the electric company. He wants to do repair work.

The interviewer asks Pete this question.

Interviewer. Do you use drugs?

Choose the answer you think Pete should give. Put an X in front of the answer you choose.

____1. No. I don't use drugs.

____2. I used to take pills. I took them when I was in high school. But I don't use any drugs now.

The first answer is the one Pete should give. He tells the interviewer the truth. He does not use drugs. Pete doesn't need to say that he took pills five years ago. Pete was smart to stop using drugs. And he never got in trouble with the police. He never got in trouble for using drugs. What Pete did in the past is finished. What he does right now is important.

Do you have one of these problems? Or do you have another problem? If you do, you may have to answer a question about it. A question about a problem may be hard to answer. Think about your answer before the interview.

Checking Facts from the Lesson

Put an X in front of each correct statement.

_____1. The interviewer asks if you have ever been convicted of a crime. You were convicted once. You should tell the truth about this.

_____2. You have not had a full-time job for two years. The interviewer asks you about this. You should not answer the question.

_____3. It is not important to tell the truth at an interview.

_____4. Your old employers may be good references.

Using Words from the Lesson

Write the correct words in the blanks below. Use these words.

checker   skill
convicted   hire

1. You know how to type. This is a _____.

2. A person is found guilty of a crime. The person has been

_____.

3. A _____ takes your money when you pay for groceries.

4. You want to give the interviewer reasons to _____ you.

Drawing Conclusions

Write Yes or No in front of each question.

_____1. You want to be a security guard. You were once convicted of stealing. But you tell the interviewer you were never convicted of a crime. Is this a good thing to do?

_____2. You dropped out of high school when you were sixteen. Now you are twenty-two. You are back in school. You will graduate soon. Should you tell this to an interviewer?

_____3. You worked part-time when your child was young. You had to take care of her. Now you are applying for a full-time job. The interviewer may ask you why you did not work full-time. Should you think about how you might answer this question?

Turn to page 62 and check your answers.

Lesson 8

Questions You May Not Have to Answer

Carlos Montez has a job interview. He wants a job building garages. Carlos is qualified for the job. He is a carpenter. A carpenter builds things out of wood. Carlos was arrested once fifteen years ago. But he was not convicted.

The interviewer asks Carlos this question.

Interviewer. Have you ever been arrested?

   Carlos. Yes. I was arrested one time. But I wasn't convicted.

Carlos does not get the job. Carlos thinks that he did not get the job because he was arrested. He also thinks that he did not have to answer the question. Did Carlos have to answer the question?

Carlos did _not_ have to say that he was arrested once. An arrest is not a conviction. The arrest has nothing to do with his qualifications as a carpenter. And the arrest should not keep Carlos from getting the job.

This lesson is about some questions you may not have to answer at an interview. The lesson tells you why you should be careful if you _do_ answer these questions.

Important Words Used in This Lesson

job discrimination Job discrimination means that an employer does not hire you for unfair reasons. The reasons are unfair if they do not have to do with your qualifications for a job. An employer might not hire someone because the person was once arrested. An employer might not hire someone because of the color of the person's skin. These are examples of job discrimination. An arrest has nothing to do with qualifications for a job. Skin color is not a qualification for a job. Job discrimination is against the law.

Carlos does not have to give information about being arrested. But how should he answer the question about arrests? Put an X in front of the answer you think Carlos should give.

_____1. You can't ask me that. It's against the law.

_____2. What does that have to do with my qualifications?

_____3. I don't think the question has anything to do with my qualifications. But I have never been convicted of a crime. And I have the qualifications for this job.

The third answer is the one Carlos should give. He doesn't give information about his arrest. But he tells the interviewer that he was never convicted of a crime. Carlos also says that he is qualified for the job.

The first answer is not correct. The interviewer can ask Carlos the question. The law does not stop an employer or interviewer from asking a question about arrests. The law says something different. It says the information in the answer cannot be used to discriminate against a person. Discriminate means to choose one person over another for unfair reasons.

The second answer is not a good answer. It doesn't sound friendly. Remember, Carlos wants the job. He doesn't have to give information about his arrest. But Carlos doesn't need to make the interviewer angry.

Question. An interviewer may ask many questions. How can you know what questions to answer?

Answer. Always ask yourself if a question has to do with your qualifications for the job. You don't have to answer a question that doesn't have to do with qualifications for the job. Your answer may be used to discriminate against you. But be careful. A question may be important for one kind of job. The same question may not be important for another kind of job.

Sometimes two questions may seem to be the same. But they are really different. Here is an example.

Margaret Mason has an interview for a job. The job is at a tool company. The person who gets the job has to lift heavy boxes all day.

The interviewer wants to ask Margaret about her health. The interviewer needs to know if Margaret will be able to do the work. Here are two questions. Put an X in front of the question that has to do with qualifications for the job.

_____1. How is your health?

_____2. Do you have any health problems that will stop you from doing this job?

The second question has to do with the job. Margaret will lift heavy boxes if she gets the job. The interviewer must know if Margaret can do that. But the interviewer does not need other health information. The information might be used to discriminate against Margaret.

Let's say the interviewer asks Margaret the first question. The interviewer asks Margaret about her general health. How should Margaret answer the question? Put an X in front of the answer you think Margaret should give.

_____1. I really don't have to give you that information.

_____2. I have no health problems that will stop me from doing this job.

The second answer is the better one. The first answer is correct. Margaret doesn't have to give all of her health information. But this answer may make the interviewer angry. Margaret doesn't want to do this.

Margaret should give the second answer. She answers the question the interviewer should have asked. The interviewer needs to know about health problems that have to do with the job.

Margaret is right to be careful. She does not want to give information that might be used to discriminate against her.

Job discrimination is against the law. But job discrimination is hard to prove. You may think an employer discriminated against you. Then you should get legal help. Legal means having to do with the law. There is important information about job discrimination on pages 53 and 54. The information will tell you how to get legal help.

Here is a list of questions. They usually don't have to do with qualifications for a job. But an interviewer might ask you some of the questions. Think about how you would answer them. You should be careful about the information you give.

- What work does your spouse do? Your spouse is your husband or wife. The work your spouse does usually has nothing to do with your qualifications.

- Do you have any children? Your children usually do not have anything to do with your job qualifications. Having children might make it hard to get to work sometimes. You might not find baby-sitters. But you might have good child care. You might be at work on time every day.

- Do you plan to have children? This information usually has nothing to do with the job. And your plans can change.

- How tall are you? Sometimes this information is important. Usually it's not. You should decide if the question has to do with the job. Then you can decide how to answer the question.

- How much do you weigh? Sometimes this information is important. Usually it's not. Decide if the question has to do with the job. Then decide how to answer the question.

- Where were you born? This information is almost never important as a qualification. You may be from a different country. Or you may be from a different part of this country. But where you were born does not help you do a job. And it does not stop you from doing a job.

- Where are your parents from? Your parents may be from a different country. Or they may be from a different part of this country. This information has nothing to do with your job qualifications.

- How old are you? Your age usually has nothing to do with your job qualifications. You should get the job if you have the best qualifications for it.

- What is your race? Your race has nothing to do with your qualifications for a job.

- What is your religion? Your religion has nothing to do with your qualifications for a job.

Checking Facts from the Lesson

Put an X in front of each correct statement.

_____1. Job discrimination is hard to prove.

_____2. You have to answer questions about your religion at an interview.

_____3. An interviewer asks where your parents were born. You do not have to give this information.

_____4. Your race is a job qualification.

Using Words from the Lesson

Write the correct words in the blanks below. Use these words.

legal   spouse
job discrimination   qualification

1. Your husband or wife is your _____.

2. Someone will not give you a job for unfair reasons. This may be

_____.

3. _____ means having to do with the law.

4. Your age is usually not a job _____.

Drawing Conclusions

Write Yes or No in front of each question.

_____1. Your mother and father are from Mexico. Does this information have anything to do with your job qualifications?

_____2. You are a woman. You have three children. An interviewer says the company does not hire women with children. Might this be job discrimination?

_____3. You think you have been discriminated against. You think you can prove this by yourself. Is it a good idea to get legal help anyway?

_____4. You apply for a job as a salesclerk. You would have to stand on your feet most of the day. You have a health problem that makes it hard for you to stand so long. The interviewer asks if you have any health problems that would stop you from doing the job. Should you tell the interviewer about your problem?

Turn to page 63 and check your answers.

Planning Your Answers

Are you ready to answer the questions interviewers may ask? Your answers are important. Interviewers learn about you by the way you answer their questions.

Your answers should be honest. And you should give exact information. For example, you should know the dates that you worked at other jobs.

Your answers should also be directed to the questions. This means that you answer the question you are asked. You do not start to talk about other things.

Form 4 has a list of interview questions. Form 4 is on pages 45 and 46. You probably will not be asked all of these questions. But you should be prepared to answer them.

You can copy Form 4. Write your answer to each question. Give answers that tell the good things about you. You should look at the form before you go to an interview. Think about your answers again. This will help you be ready to answer questions.

You can prepare for an interview in another way. Fill out the form. Then ask a friend to act as an interviewer. You can say you are applying for a certain job. Your friend can ask you some questions on the form. You should answer the questions aloud.

Do not read your answers from the form. You will not read them at an interview. Give the answers the way you would talk to an interviewer. You need to remember the information. But you can give the information in different ways at each interview.

Write your answers to the questions on Form 4.

Interview Questions—Form 4

PERSONAL INFORMATION

1. Have you ever been convicted of a crime? _____

_____

2. Can you prove your age if you are hired? _____

3. What are your hobbies and interests? _____

_____

EDUCATION

1. Where did you go to high school? _____

2. Did you finish high school? _____

_____

3. Do you plan to finish high school? _____

_____

4. Do you have any college education? _____

_____

5. What vocational or skill training have you had? _____

_____

QUALIFICATIONS AND SKILLS

1. What are your qualifications for the job? _____

_____

2. What kinds of work have you done before? _____

_____

3. Do you know how to run any machines? What are they? _____

_____

4. What did you learn to do at your last job? _____

_____

5. Have you had any experience supervising people? What kind of experience have you had?

_____

6. What are three things you do well? _____

_____

REFERENCES AND JOB EXPERIENCE

1. Do you have references? What are the names and addresses of your references? _____

_____

_____

2. Where have you worked before? List the names of places you have worked. _____

_____

WORK RECORD

1. Why weren't you working for some time? (Answer this question only if you did not work for

some time.) _____

_____

2. Why did you leave your last job? _____

_____

3. What did you like most about your last job? _____

_____

4. What did you like least about your last job? _____

_____

HEALTH

1. Do you have any health problems that will stop you from doing the job? _____

_____

2. Do you use drugs? _____

GENERAL INFORMATION

1. Why do you want this job? _____

_____

2. Why should I give you this job? _____

_____

3. Why would you like to work for this company? _____

_____

4. What kinds of work don't you like? _____

5. What are your vocational plans? _____

_____

Checking Facts from the Lesson

Put an X in front of each correct statement.

_____1. You should be honest when you answer questions at an interview.

_____2. An interviewer asks you a question. You can start to talk about other things.

_____3. An interviewer may ask questions about your education.

_____4. You should not read your answers from a form.

Using Words from the Lesson

Write the correct words in the blanks below. Use these words.

education   prepared
health   reference

1. Your last employer liked your work. The employer can be a good

   _____.

2. You will be asked questions at an interview. You should be

   _____ to answer them.

3. You may have plans to finish your high school _____.

4. Poor eyesight is a _____ problem that an interviewer may ask about.

Drawing Conclusions

Write Yes or No in front of each question.

_____1. The interviewer asks when you finished high school. You say that you graduated many years ago. Is this a good answer?

_____2. The interviewer asks where you learned to type. You say that you learned to type in high school. You say that you did not like your teacher. Is this a good answer to the question?

_____3. You know that your teacher and your last employer will give you good references. Do you need to get their names and addresses before you have an interview?

Turn to page 63 and check your answers.

Lesson 10

You Are an Interviewer, Too

A job interviewer gets information about you. But you need information, too. There are questions you will have to ask at some interviews. You will have to be an interviewer. You need information to help you decide if you want the job.

This lesson tells you about some questions you may want to ask. It tells you about information you should get. You should find out the answers before you take a job.

Important Words Used in This Lesson

---

pension A pension is money paid to someone who has retired, or stopped working. The person has retired because of age, illness, or an accident. A pension is usually paid by a company. Sometimes it is paid by the government. Not all companies pay pensions. Not all people get pensions.

profit sharing Profit is the money a company has left after it pays all its expenses. Expenses are amounts of money a company spends to stay in business. Rent is an expense. Salaries are an expense. Sometimes companies give part of their profits to the employees. This is called profit sharing. Not all companies have profit sharing.

union A union is a group of workers who are joined together to get things they want. Unions help workers get good salaries and benefits. There are many different unions. They are for people who do different kinds of jobs. Not all employees belong to unions. But you must join a union if you want to get certain jobs. Joining a union costs money. Unions are sometimes called labor unions.

The questions you ask at an interview are important. You need information about the job and the employer. How you ask for the information is also important. This lesson will show you why.

Here are some important questions you should ask at a job interview.

What does the job pay?

Let's say the interviewer doesn't tell you the salary for the job. You need this information. Below are some questions about salary. Put an X in front of each question you think is a good one to ask.

_____ 1. Does this job pay much?

_____ 2. How much does this job pay?

_____ 3. Could you tell me the salary for this job?

Number 2 and number 3 are good questions to ask. Number 1 is not a friendly way to ask. You should ask questions in a friendly way. You do not want to make the interviewer angry.

What benefits does the employer give?

Benefits are important. Some employers give many benefits. Some give few benefits. Let's say an employer has an insurance plan. You want to know about the plan. How do you find out about it? Put an X in front of the best question or statement to use.

_____ 1. I understand the company has an insurance plan. Would you tell me about the plan? And would you tell me who pays for it?

_____ 2. Tell me about the insurance plan. It's important to me.

_____ 3. Is your insurance plan any good?

Number 1 is the best. You show that you know about the insurance plan. But you ask the interviewer to tell you more about it.

Number 2 is not good. You are telling the interviewer what to do. Most people don't like to be told what to do. It is better to ask a question. But number 3 is not a good question. It does not sound friendly.

What are the chances for promotion?

Chances for promotion may be important to you. Can you get a better job later with the same company? Can you learn new skills while you work for the company? These are important questions. How would you ask for the information? Put an X in front of the best question or questions to ask.

_____ 1. How do I get a better job in this company?

_____ 2. Do you give people a chance to learn new skills?

_____ 3. Are there good chances for promotion in the company? Does the company have any training programs to teach people new skills?

Number 3 is the best. You ask direct questions. You ask about certain things. This is better than general questions like number 1 and number 2.

Here is one more question you might have to ask. It is a very important question.

How do I find out if I get the job?

Let's say the interview is over. You are ready to leave. But the interviewer has not told you if you have the job. Or the interviewer has not decided who will get the job. You don't know how or when you will find out about the job. It is important to get this information. What should you say? Put an X in front of the best question to ask.

_____1. Should I call you in a day or two to see if I have the job?

_____2. How will I find out if I have the job?

_____3. Will you call me to let me know about the job?

Number 1 is the best question to ask. You show the interviewer that the job is important to you. You will make a call. You won't just wait for the interviewer to call you. The interviewer may have a different way to let you know about the job. But your question shows that you really want the job.

The interviewer may not give you all the information you want. You should ask for this information if it is important to you.

- Ask for a job description. A job description tells what someone must do on a certain job. A job description can be spoken or written.

- Ask about the working hours. What hours will you have to work?

- Ask about a union. Will you have to join a union? How much will it cost?

- Ask about vacation. How much vacation time will you get each year? Will you be paid for vacation time? When can you take your vacation?

- Ask about your supervisor. If you get the job, who will be your supervisor? What is the name of the supervisor?

- Ask about a pension plan. Does the company have a pension plan? How does the plan work?

- Ask about profit sharing. Does the company have profit sharing? How does the profit sharing work?

Use Form 5 on page 51 to write down information about the job and the employer. Copy the form. Make as many copies as you think you will need. Take a copy to each job interview. The form will help you remember what questions to ask.

You can write down some answers at the interview. But do not write a lot. It is better to listen to the interviewer. You can remember most of the answers. You can fill out the form after your interview. Then you won't forget the information.

Information About the Job and the Employer—Form 5

NAME OF EMPLOYER _____

ADDRESS _____

NAME OF INTERVIEWER _____

JOB TITLE (KIND OF JOB) _____

JOB DESCRIPTION _____

_____

SALARY _____

WORKING HOURS _____

CHANCES FOR PROMOTION _____

_____

BENEFITS

Circle Yes or No for each benefit. Then fill in the blanks with other information you may get.

Training Program	Yes	No	Important Information _____
			_____
Health Insurance	Yes	No	Cost _____
			Who pays? _____
Life Insurance	Yes	No	Cost _____
			Who pays? _____
Vacation	Yes	No	How long? _____
			Will you be paid? _____
Pension Plan	Yes	No	Important Information _____
			_____
Profit Sharing	Yes	No	Important Information _____
			_____

Will you have to join a union? _____ How much will it cost? _____

How and when will you find out if you have the job? _____

_____

Do you want to work for this employer? _____ Why? _____

_____

Other Information _____

_____

Checking Facts from the Lesson

Put an X in front of each correct statement.

_____1. You can ask questions at a job interview.

_____2. You should ask about insurance only after you have worked at a job for some time.

_____3. You should ask about the salary for a job. You should ask if the interviewer does not tell you.

_____4. You should not ask an interviewer about training programs.

Using Words from the Lesson

Write the correct words in the blanks below. Use these words.

    pension   job description
    union   profit

1. A _____ is money paid to someone who has retired.

2. A _____ can be written or spoken.

3. _____ is the money a company has left after it pays all its expenses.

4. You may have to join a _____ if you want to get certain jobs.

Drawing Conclusions

Write Yes or No in front of each question.

_____1. The interviewer does not tell you about a union. But your friend works at the company. He belongs to a union. Should you ask the interviewer about unions?

_____2. You are at a job interview. You are very interested in the company's pension plan. The interviewer does not tell you about the plan. Should you ask the interviewer about the plan?

_____3. Your interview is over. But the interviewer has not told you when you will hear about the job. You leave without asking when you will hear. Is this a good thing to do?

Turn to page 63 and check your answers.

What to Do About Job Discrimination

You think that an employer has discriminated against you. What can you do? You can phone or visit people and places that can help you. Ask them what the law says. Ask them what you can do.

You may be right. The employer may have discriminated against you. But you may be wrong. Or you may not be able to prove that there was discrimination against you. Get help from someone who knows the law.

Here is a list of people and places that can help you. The list tells you how to look up the people and places in the telephone book. You can get the phone number and address of each person or place.

1. A lawyer can help you. A lawyer is a person who knows the law. Attorney is another word for lawyer. The services of a lawyer may cost a lot of money. You can use the white pages of the telephone book to find a lawyer. Use them if you know the name of the lawyer. You can also use the Yellow Pages. Look under the heading **Lawyers** or **Attorneys.**

2. A legal aid or legal assistance group can help you. Legal means having to do with law. Aid and assistance mean help. Legal aid and legal assistance groups give legal help.

   Use the white pages if you know the name of a group. You can look under Legal Aid Bureau, Legal Aid Society, or Legal Assistance Foundation. These are the names of some legal aid groups.

You can also use the Yellow Pages. Look for a heading that begins with **Legal.** Or look under **Social Service Organizations.** Read the names of the groups. You may find the word legal in some names. Then you can phone one of the groups. Ask if the group can help you.

3. The United States Equal Employment Opportunity Commission can help you.

   Use the white pages. Look under UNITED STATES GOVERNMENT. Then find the listing for EQUAL EMPLOYMENT OPPORTUNITY COMMISSION. This place is listed under United States Government.

4. Your state Equal Employment Opportunity Commission can help you. This office may have a different name in your state. It may be called the Fair Employment Practices Commission. Your state may have a human rights commission. Or it may have an affirmative action office.

   Use the white pages. Look up the name of your state. Then look under each name given above. For example, look under Equal Employment Opportunity Commission. If you don't find a listing, look under Fair Employment Practices Commission. Look until you find a listing.

5. Your city may have an office that can help you. It is a good idea to look in the white pages. Look up the name of your city. If you live in Marshall, look up Marshall—City of. Then look under Equal Employment Opportunity Commission. If you don't find a listing, look under Fair Employment Practices Commission or Human Rights Commission or Affirmative Action Office.

Job discrimination is hard to prove. It is hard to prove that an employer has broken a law. You need help from someone who knows the law.

Activities

Activity 1

Interviewers may use special words at an interview. It is important for you to know what the words mean.

Here are some of these words and their meanings. Look at each word. Then look at the meanings. Find the meaning for the word. Write the letter of the meaning in the blank next to the word. The first blank is filled in for you.

salary _d_

benefit _c_

pension _j_

union _g_

products _h_

hobbies _f_

qualification _b_

promotion _i_

skill _e_

references _a_

a. people who can give information about you

b. anything that makes you able to do a job

c. an extra thing you get besides your pay

d. money you get for doing a job

e. something you can do because you have training or experience

f. things you like to do in your free time

g. a special group of workers who are joined together

h. things a company makes or grows to sell

i. a better job in the place where you work

j. money paid to someone who has retired

Turn to page 64 and check your answers.

Don Newman has a job interview. Here is some information about the interview. Read the information. Look for the things Don does right at the interview. Look for the things he does wrong. Then answer the questions that follow the information.

Don's Interview

Don has a job interview at ten o'clock. He is applying for a job as a salesclerk. Don takes a bus to the store. He arrives a few minutes early. He fills out an application. Someone in the personnel office tells Don to go into the office of the interviewer. The interviewer is talking on the phone. She points to a chair. She wants Don to sit down and wait for her.

Don sits down quietly. He opens the buttons on his heavy winter coat. He does not take off his coat. Don sees an ashtray on the desk. He lights a cigarette.

The interviewer finishes her call. She is ready to talk to Don. The interviewer tells Don her name is Sue Smith. Don calls her Miss Smith when he answers questions. He acts friendly.

The interviewer asks Don about his job experience. Don knows the names of the companies where he worked. He knows the dates that he worked at the companies. But Don does not remember the names of his supervisors.

The interviewer reads Don's application. Don talks about how much he wants the job. He talks while the interviewer is reading. Don answers Miss Smith's questions. His answers are complete. He gives extra information sometimes. Don does this when he thinks it will help him get the job.

When the interview is over, Don stands up. He says good-bye. He shakes hands with Miss Smith.

Here are questions about Don's interview. Write <u>Yes</u> or <u>No</u> in front of each question.

_____ 1. Was Don smart to arrive a few minutes early?

_____ 2. Was it right for Don to sit down in the office?

_____ 3. Was it good for Don to wear his coat at the interview?

_____ 4. Was it smart for Don to smoke?

_____ 5. Was it good to call the interviewer Miss Smith?

_____ 6. Was it good for Don to act friendly?

_____ 7. Should Don have known the names of his supervisors?

_____ 8. Was it smart for Don to talk while the interviewer was reading?

_____ 9. Was it smart to give complete answers?

_____10. Was it good for Don to give extra information?

_____11. Was it good for Don to shake hands with Miss Smith when he left?

Turn to page 64 and check your answers.

Lucy Lopez and Robert Berg are going to job interviews. Read the information about their appearance. Decide if each person is dressed right for the interview. Then answer the questions after the information.

Lucy Lopez

Lucy applies for a job in a department store. She wants to be a salesclerk. She wears a brown dress to the interview. She wears high-heeled shoes. Lucy wears a lot of jewelry. She wears three rings and four bracelets. Lucy's hair is short and neat.

Answer these questions. Write <u>Yes</u> or <u>No</u> in front of each question.

_____1. Should a salesclerk wear high-heeled shoes?

_____2. Lucy wears four bracelets and three rings. Should she wear that much jewelry?

_____3. Lucy wears a dress to the interview. Her hair is short and neat. Will these things make a good impression on the interviewer?

Robert Berg

Robert applies for a job in a restaurant. He would seat people at tables in the restaurant. So Robert will meet people all the time. He wears a sports jacket and pants to the interview. His shoes are new. Robert's shirt needs to be ironed. His tie is out of date. Most people don't wear ties like that anymore.

Answer these questions. Write <u>Yes</u> or <u>No</u> in front of each question.

_____1. Robert wears a sports jacket and new shoes to the interview. Does this clothing show the interviewer that Robert cares about getting the job?

_____2. Robert's tie is out of date. His shirt is not ironed. Will these things make a good impression on the interviewer?

_____3. The person who gets the job will meet many people. Is it important to look neat for the job?

Turn to page 64 and check your answers.

Activity 4

Be ready to answer all the questions an interviewer asks. Your answers should be friendly and honest. Remember, there is some information that you do not have to give. You should give the information only if it will help you get the job.

Below are some questions an interviewer might ask. You will choose the best way to answer each question.

You apply for a job lifting boxes. The boxes must be moved from the floor to a high shelf. You are not very tall. You don't weigh very much. The interviewer asks you these questions.

Interviewer. How tall are you? How much do you weigh?

Choose the answer you think is the best one. Put an X in front of the answer you choose.

_____ 1. Those questions do not have anything to do with my qualifications for the job.

_____ 2. I am tall enough to do the job, and I weigh enough. I can reach the shelf easily. I will be happy to put some boxes on the shelf. Then you will see that I can do the job.

_____ 3. I am tall enough to reach the shelf. I think I weigh enough to lift the boxes, too.

You apply for a job as a typist. Your parents are from Puerto Rico. The interviewer says you must speak and write English well to do the job. Your English is good. The interviewer asks you this question.

Interviewer. Where are your parents from?

Choose the answer you think is the best one. Put an X in front of the answer you choose.

_____ 1. My parents were born in the United States.

_____ 2. My parents are from Puerto Rico. But that information has nothing to do with my English.

_____ 3. Maybe you are interested in my English. I speak English well. I learned it in school. I also write and spell well. I would be happy to take tests to show you that I speak and write well.

Turn to page 64 and check your answers.

Lesson 1

1. The next day, or tomorrow
2. Nine o'clock in the morning
3. Clark Coat Company
4. 419 West May Street
5. Room 125
6. Mrs. Herrod

Lesson 3

Cynthia Ayala

No
No

Allan Partee

Yes
Yes

Lesson 6

What skills did you learn from your last job?

1.
2. X

Why did you leave your last job?

1.
2.
3. X

What are your goals for the next few years?

1.
2. X

Answers to Exercises

Checking Facts from the Lesson	**Using Words from the Lesson**	**Drawing Conclusions**

Lesson 1

1. X	1. employer	1. No. The time is important. Ask for it.
2.	2. interviewer	2. Yes. The person or company you work for is your employer.
3.	3. personnel office	3. Yes. You won't know where to go unless you call.
4. X	4. job interview	4. Yes. It is good to know the name of the interviewer.

Lesson 2

1. X	1. job application	1. Yes. The teacher and the employer can be good references.
2. X	2. References	2. Yes. It is good to show that you know what the company makes.
3. X	3. Services	3. No. The job application may ask for the dates. Or the interviewer may ask.
4.	4. Manufacture	4. Yes. Then you can show the interviewer your interest in the company.

Lesson 3

1. X	1. appearance	1. No. A suit is OK. Clean work pants and a shirt are also OK.
2.	2. uniforms	2. No. Interviewers like people to be neat and clean.
3. X	3. applies	3. Yes. You want to look neat. Shave off the beard.
4.	4. qualifications	4. Yes. Nancy should not wear fancy clothing. But a plain skirt is fine.

Checking Facts from the Lesson	Using Words from the Lesson	Drawing Conclusions
1.	1. benefit	1. Yes. The interviewer will know that you would not have problems getting to work.
2. X	2. products	2. Yes. You have a good reference. This may help you get the job.
3. X	3. skill	3. Yes. Tell the interviewer about skills that will help you do the job.
4. X	4. Employees	4. No. The length of the interview is not always important.
5.		

Lesson 5

1.	1. prepared	1. Yes. Interviewers like to look at your whole face. Tell why you must wear the sunglasses.
2. X	2. impression	2. No. You should call the interviewer. Ask if you can change the interview to another time.
3. X	3. interviewer	3. No. The interviewer may think that you don't care about the job.
4.	4. Social Security	

Lesson 6

1. X	1. goal	1. Yes. It shows that you are interested in your work.
2.	2. promotion	2. No. You should tell the interviewer about your work plans.
3. X	3. supervisor	3. Yes. This experience could help you do the job.
4.	4. salary	4. No. You should have some idea of what your work is worth.
5. X		

Lesson 7

1. X	1. skill	1. No. The interviewer can check your record. You may be fired if you lie.
2.	2. convicted	2. Yes. It shows that you know an education is important.
3.	3. checker	3. Yes. Think about your answer before the interview.
4. X	4. hire	

Checking Facts from the Lesson	**Using Words from the Lesson**	**Drawing Conclusions**
1. X 2. 3. X 4.	1. spouse 2. job discrimination 3. Legal 4. qualification	1. No. The information has nothing to do with your qualifications. 2. Yes. This is usually job discrimination. 3. Yes. You need help because discrimination is hard to prove. 4. Yes. The interviewer has a right to know about health problems that have to do with the job.
Lesson 9		
1. X 2. 3. X 4. X	1. reference 2. prepared 3. education 4. health	1. No. It is better to give the year that you graduated. 2. No. Just tell where you learned to type. The other information is not helpful. 3. Yes. Then the interviewer can get in touch with them.
Lesson 10		
1. X 2. 3. X 4.	1. pension 2. job description 3. Profit 4. union	1. Yes. You may have to join a union. This would cost money. 2. Yes. You can ask about benefits that are important to you. 3. No. You need the information. And the interviewer may think that you don't care about the job.

Answers to Activities

Activity 1

c
j
g
h
f
b
i
e
a

Activity 2

1. Yes
2. Yes
3. No
4. No
5. Yes
6. Yes
7. Yes
8. No
9. Yes
10. Yes
11. Yes

Activity 3

Lucy Lopez

1. No
2. No
3. Yes

Robert Berg

1. Yes
2. No
3. Yes

Activity 4

1.
2. X
3.

1.
2.
3. X